This edition published by Parragon Books Ltd in 2017

Parragon Books Ltd
Chartist House
15–17 Trim Street
Bath BA1 1HA, UK
www.parragon.com

ISBN 978-1-4748-6209-7

Printed in China

Disney
My First
Picture
Encyclopedia

Learning is fun with your Disney friends

PaRragon

Bath · New York · Cologne · Melbourne · Delhi
Hong Kong · Shenzhen · Singapore

A note for parents

Young children absorb facts and information at an astonishing rate. Curious pre-schoolers and children just starting school learn more in their first five years than at any other time in their lives.

This Disney First Picture Encyclopedia has been designed to complement and enhance this unique period in your child's development. It offers a friendly, age-appropriate introduction to animals, nature and the wider world around us. All along the way, favourite Disney characters appear to make your child's learning entertaining and fun.

Here are some handy tips on how to use this book:

● The information in the Encyclopedia is layered, providing a rich learning experience without overwhelming your child. Pore over the photographs, read out the words, labels and captions, and enjoy the facts in the colourful 'Did you know?' boxes.

● Ask questions as you look at the pages, encouraging your child to use context to work out their answer. If they get the question wrong, don't worry – eliminating wrong answers and then searching for the right one together is a great way to learn.

● Allow your child to direct the reading experience, taking you to the pages that appeal to them. Use the information as a starting point for lively discussion, encouraging your child to go off-page and explore subjects that interest them in more depth.

● When you encounter an interesting animal, unusual weather or a new vehicle in your daily life, build on this experience when you get home. Show your child how to use the contents and index pages to look up specific topics. Although your child may not be reading yet, finding out how reference books work will help them to model this behaviour later on.

● Keep reading sessions short. Your child might want to pore over an entire chapter, or just dip in and point at a picture. Both are fine. When they start to get tired, put the book down until next time.

The Disney First Picture Encyclopedia will help set your child on a lifelong learning adventure. Enjoy sharing it together!

Contents

Mammals

We share our planet with millions of animals – from tiny insects to soaring birds and huge, deep-sea fish. You are an animal, too. Humans are one of the 5,000 different types of mammal on Earth.

What are mammals?

Mammals are warm-blooded animals, which means their bodies stay about the same temperature most of the time. Mammals have hair or fur.

This mother cheetah has three cubs.

A baby is born

Most mammals do not hatch from eggs – they grow inside their mothers instead. Baby mammals feed on their mothers' milk.

Dog

A dog is a type of mammal that lives in many of our homes. It is often called 'man's best friend'. Dogs are loyal and easy to train.

A pair of golden retriever puppies.

Puppy power

Baby dogs are called puppies. For the first two weeks of life, they cannot see or hear. All puppies are born with blue eyes, but most change colour after a month or two.

Dogs come in all **shapes** and sizes! This is a beagle.

Woof! Woof!

Rabbit

Rabbits live in many places, from swamps and woodlands to forests and deserts. Their long ears can turn in any direction, helping them hear even the faintest sounds.

Snuggle up!

Rabbits live together in groups in underground burrows. Baby rabbits do not have fur when they are born, so they must snuggle together to stay warm.

Rabbits use their **twitchy** noses to sniff out tasty plants to eat.

Thump!
Thump!

Thump and go

Rabbits thump their hind legs to let other rabbits know when they sense danger.

Horse

Horses are large, strong mammals with hooves and long manes and tails. Some people use horses for riding, while others use them to pull or carry heavy loads.

Male foals are called colts. Female foals are called fillies.

Wobbly walkers

Baby horses are called foals. Foals are born with very long legs compared to their bodies, so their walking is a bit wobbly at first.

Did you know?

Horses can lock the joints in their legs into a standing position so they can sleep upright without falling over!

Say cheese!

By the age of six to nine months, foals will have all their baby teeth. A horse's adult teeth won't all come through until it is five years old.

Horses **neigh** and **snort** to show how they are feeling.

Elephant

There are two types of elephant – the African elephant has large ears, while Asian elephants have ears that are smaller and rounder.

The African elephant is the **largest** land mammal.

Top trunk

An elephant uses its trunk for breathing, smelling and picking up food. When it needs a wash, it can suck water into its trunk and then hose itself down.

Stomp! Stomp!

Asian elephants having fun in the **mud**.

Fancy a mud bath?

An elephant's wrinkly skin is very sensitive. To keep their skin cool and protect it from sunburn and insect bites, elephants roll around in the mud.

Chimpanzee

Chimpanzees are our closest relatives. They show their feelings in the same way that humans do. They hug, kiss, smile and even tickle each other when they're playing!

Super swingers

Chimpanzees have very long arms, which they use to swing from tree branches and vines in the forests where they live.

Chimps have **powerful** arms and legs, but no tail.

Chimpanzees are good at working things out.

Sticks and stones

Unlike most animals, chimpanzees are able to make and use tools. They use rocks to crack open nuts and mash up fruit, and they use sticks to catch ants and termites.

Kangaroo

Kangaroos are a type of mammal called a marsupial. Their tummies have pouches that they use to carry their babies around in. Kangaroos live in Australia.

This red kangaroo's **tail** is long and super-strong.

Two legs or three?

A kangaroo uses its tail as an extra leg, pushing it forward as it hops along. The tail also helps the kangaroo to balance when it is standing or kicking.

These kangaroos live in the Blue Mountains in Australia.

Little roos

Baby kangaroos are called joeys. A joey will feed and grow in its mother's pouch for almost one year.

Did you know?

When they are born, joeys are about the size of a human thumb!

Hummingbird

Hummingbirds are the smallest birds in the world – some are even shorter than a playing card! The tiny creatures fly from flower to flower, using their long beaks to sip the nectar from inside.

Hover and fly

Hummingbirds can move their wings in a circle. They are the only birds that are able to fly upwards, downwards, forwards, backwards and sideways.

Some hummingbirds have **shimmery** feathers.

There are over 300 types of hummingbird.

Did you know?

Hummingbirds collect nectar from as many as 1,000 flowers in a single day!

Ostrich

The ostrich is the largest bird in the world. Although it cannot fly, the ostrich can run faster than any other bird alive.

Back off!

If an ostrich feels threatened, it kicks out its leg. Ostriches use their strong and powerful kick to protect themselves against animals such as lions.

Ostriches can run for long distances.

Did you know?

Ostrich eggs are big and heavy. Each one is about the size of 24 chicken eggs!

This ostrich is a metre **taller** than most grown-up people!

Penguin

Most penguins are black and white. The birds are excellent swimmers, using their wings to paddle through the ocean and to keep their balance as they waddle across icy rocks.

A gentoo penguin sits on its egg.

Emperor penguin chicks have **fuzzy** grey feathers.

Taking turns

Female penguins usually lay one egg at a time. Male and female penguins take it in turns to look after the egg. A female penguin will often go hunting for food while the male keeps the egg warm.

We are family

A group of penguins living together is called a rookery. Living side-by-side in large numbers allows the penguins to huddle together and stay warm.

Reptiles and amphibians

Both reptiles and amphibians are cold-blooded. This means that their bodies are the same temperature as their surroundings. Most reptiles and amphibians hatch from eggs.

Snakes **slither** on scaly skin.

What are reptiles?
Reptiles are animals that are covered with scales. Scales are rough, dry pieces of skin that protect a reptile's body.

What are amphibians?
Amphibians are animals that don't have hair, fur, feathers or scales. They have wet, smooth skin. Most amphibians live in or around water because they must keep their skin moist.

This tree frog lives in the **damp** rainforest.

Chameleon

Chameleons are reptiles. They can change the shade of their skin to almost any colour of the rainbow. This helps them to hide when an enemy comes near.

Slurp!

Can you see me now?

Brilliant bug catchers

Chameleons have long, sticky tongues. They flick them out to catch passing insects.

Did you know?

These colourful lizards can turn their eyes in any direction. They can even look behind them without moving their heads!

Giant tortoise

The giant tortoise has a hard, plated shell to protect its body. It's a massive reptile that can weigh more than two fully grown men! It grazes on shrubs, grasses and even cacti.

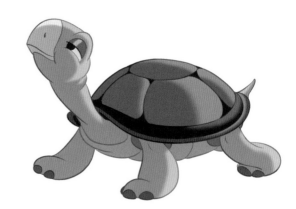

Tortoises have a **strong** mouth, but no teeth.

Ancient animals

The giant tortoise is one of the longest-living creatures on Earth. Many live to over 100 years old, but some make it to 150 and beyond.

This tortoise has **pulled** in its head.

Hide-and-seek

Unlike turtles, a giant tortoise spends its life on land. If it feels afraid, the tortoise pulls its head, neck and legs back into its hard shell. It doesn't come out until it feels safe again.

Poison dart frog

The poison dart frog – also called the poison arrow frog – is an amphibian. It captures spiders, ants and termites with its long, sticky tongue.

Croak!

Croak!

This frog's bright yellow skin warns others to stay away.

Daddy daycare

The male poison dart frog cares for his babies by watching over the eggs. Once they hatch, tadpoles swim on to the dad's back, then he carries them to a safe spot where they can continue to grow.

Skin with a sting

The poison dart frog got its name from native South American tribes. They use the poison from the frogs' skin on the tips of their blowpipe darts for hunting.

Pretty, but **Poisonous!**

Sea creatures

Sea creatures are animals that live in or around the sea. Fish swim below the surface, whales leap and dive and seabirds step through the shallows. Other sea creatures, such as crabs and lobsters, scuttle along the ocean floor.

This colourful butterfly fish lives on a coral reef.

What are fish?

Fish are creatures that live in the water. They breathe through gills on either side of their throats. Most fish also have scales and fins on their bodies.

What are sea mammals?

Some sea creatures are mammals. Sea mammals can't stay underwater all the time. They have to come to the surface to breathe air.

Dolphin

Dolphins are playful sea mammals that live in family groups called pods. They stay very close to the other pod members. If a dolphin gets hurt or is in trouble, the rest of the pod will try to help it.

A mother dolphin and her calf **leap** out of the water.

Did you know?

Baby dolphins stay with their mothers for three to six years before joining a pod of other young dolphins.

Click!

Click!

Getting some air

As soon as a baby dolphin is born, it swims up to the surface to breathe in air. Afterwards, it will dive back down to drink its mother's milk.

Dolphins make noises to talk to each other.

Shark

Sharks are fish that have been on Earth for a very long time. Unlike other fish, sharks do not have bones. Sharks' skeletons are made of cartilage – the same stuff that our noses and ears are made from.

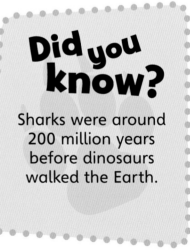

It's easy to see how the hammerhead shark got its name!

Fearsome fangs

Sharks have very sharp, bony teeth. If a tooth is damaged or lost, a shark can grow a new one. A typical shark has about 30,000 teeth throughout its lifetime.

Did you know?

Sharks were around 200 million years before dinosaurs walked the Earth.

Octopus

An octopus has eight arms and a soft, round head. Each arm is lined with suction cups, which help it to open shells and other food. If the octopus loses one of its arms, it can grow a new one!

Hank is a **septopus** - an octopus with only seven tentacles!

The octopus stretches its soft body to help it **glide** through the ocean.

Quick getaway

When they need to move fast, octopuses have a clever way of getting around. They push water out and away from their bodies to move themselves along.

Hunt and grab

The octopus uses its arms to catch crabs, fish, turtles, shrimp and other octopuses. Afterwards it injects poison into its prey through its parrot-like beak.

B gs and creepy-crawlies

The world is full of insects, spiders and bugs! Most creepy-crawlies have exoskeletons, which means that their skeletons are on the outside of their bodies.

What are arachnids?

Arachnids are animals with eight legs, such as spiders, scorpions and ticks. Their bodies only have two parts.

Dragonflies are insects that live near rivers, lakes and streams.

What are insects?

Insects are animals with six legs. Their bodies are divided into three parts. Many of them have wings and feelers.

Other crawlers

There are also plenty of animals that don't have six or eight legs. Millipedes and centipedes have between 30 and 200 legs, but worms have no legs at all!

Millipedes like **damp**, dark places.

Tarantula

The world's biggest and hairiest spider is the tarantula. Tarantulas live in warm climates such as hot, dry deserts or humid rainforests. Most live in burrows in the ground, but some live in trees.

Tarantulas have **eight** eyes, but they can't see very well.

A tarantula lifts up its front legs when startled.

Hairy and scary

Some tarantulas have hairs on their backs that they can rub off using their back legs. These hairs stick to other animals and make them very itchy!

Make way for the red-knee tarantula!

Spider bite

Tarantulas are poisonous, but their poison won't seriously harm humans. If a tarantula were to bite a human, the effect would be no worse than a bee sting.

Did you know?

Some tarantulas are as big as a dinner plate!

Butterfly

Butterflies are a type of insect. Some butterflies have brightly coloured wings to warn predators that they taste bad! Others have dull-coloured wings to help them hide.

Hungry caterpillar

A butterfly starts life as a caterpillar. It spends most of its time eating leaves and flowers. As it eats, the caterpillar gets bigger and bigger.

All wrapped up

After a while, the caterpillar's hard skin turns into a pod. It stays inside this chrysalis until it turns into a butterfly.

A monarch butterfly **growing** inside its chrysalis.

Ant

Ants are tiny insects, but they can do some incredible things. They live together in huge nests called colonies. The ant in charge of each colony is called the queen.

The queen is **bigger** than the other ants in the colony.

Let's work!

Every ant has a job to do. Workers help to build the nest or gather food. Drones mate with the queen. Soldiers use their strength to protect the colony.

Tiny farmers

There are lots of different types of ant. Leafcutter ants carry pieces of leaf back to their nest, then use them to grow fungus. This fungus provides food for the whole colony.

Age of the dinosaurs

Millions of years ago, long before there were people, dinosaurs lived on Earth. These amazing creatures came in many different shapes and sizes. Some ate other animals and some ate plants.

What were dinosaurs?

Dinosaurs belonged to a group of animals called reptiles. Some had tough scaly skin, while others had feathers, spikes, horns or beaks. Their babies hatched from eggs.

Argentinosaurus was the **biggest** dinosaur to walk on Earth.

Did you know?

Dinosaurs were around for over 150 million years. That's a long time! Modern humans have lived on Earth for less than 200,000 years.

Meat or vegetables?

We can tell whether a dinosaur was a meat-eater or a vegetarian (or both) from its teeth. Sharp, pointy teeth were good for tearing into meat, while larger, flatter teeth were good for chewing leaves.

A coprolite is fossilized **dinosaur poo!**

This tooth belonged to a **meat-eating** dinosaur.

Stinky stuff!

Fossilized dinosaur poos are known as coprolites. The remains of fish scales, leaves, stems, seeds, flesh, teeth and bits of chewed bone have been found in coprolites.

It can take months to carefully uncover a large dinosaur fossil.

Digging in the dirt

Dinosaur bones and fossils have been found all over the world. These discoveries help scientists work out where the different kinds of dinosaur lived.

Tyrannosaurus rex

The mighty Tyrannosaurus was a fierce hunter. As tall as a house and heavier than an African elephant, it roamed the forests and river valleys of North America and parts of Asia.

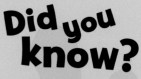
Crunch!

Crunch!

T. rex had large legs, but its arms were **tiny**.

Bone crusher

T. rex had the strongest jaws of any dinosaur. Its razor-sharp teeth could easily bite and tear the flesh and crush the bones of the animals it ate.

Dinner time

Tyrannosaurus rex had a monster appetite to match its giant size. It is thought it could eat more than 200 kilograms of meat in one bite. That's the same as eating one whole cow!

Diplodocus

Diplodocus was one of the longest dinosaurs to roam the Earth. It nearly stretched as far as three buses parked end to end! The dinosaur lived in herds and ate plants. It moved slowly on four pillar-like legs.

Swishhh!

g its back.

Diplodocus may have had **sp**

Balancing act

Diplodocus had an incredibly long neck, but its tail was longer still. The tail helped it to balance, and could also be swung around fast when Diplodocus needed to protect itself.

A Diplodocus herd could eat **massive** amounts of plants and leaves.

Toes and claws

Diplodocus had wide, five-toed elephant-like feet. Each of the four feet had a claw on one of the toes.

Ichthyosaurs

During the days of the dinosaurs, the Earth's oceans were full of giant creatures called plesiosaurs and ichthyosaurs. These strange animals were marine reptiles, with powerful jaws for snapping up fish and squid.

Ichthyosaurs had strong, pointed teeth.

Air breathers

Although ichthyosaurs had fish-like bodies, they did not have gills like a fish. They needed to come up to the surface to breathe.

Swimming champs

Ichthyosaurs were fast and strong swimmers. They used their four paddle-shaped fins and powerful fish-like tails to push and steer them through the oceans at high speeds.

Ichthyosaurs were excellent hunters.

Pteranodon

Pteranodon was a flying reptile with leathery, skin-like wings. Scientists think that it used its beak to scoop its food – mainly fish and squid – out of the ocean, like a pelican.

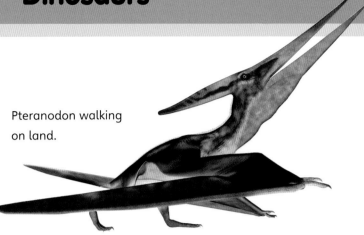

Pteranodon walking on land.

Wing and waddle

This huge creature ruled the prehistoric skies. It could also fold up its giant wings and walk upright on all fours over short distances!

Pteranodon means **winged** and **toothless**.

Did you know?

Pteranodon had light, hollow bones like a bird. This made it easier for them to lift their huge bodies into the air when they flew.

Triceratops

Triceratops lived at the same time as Tyrannosaurus rex. The horned dinosaur might have looked terrifying, but it didn't eat meat. The gentle giant fed on shrubs, ferns and palm leaves instead.

It's easy to spot a Triceratops **skull**.

Giant armoured head

Triceratops had one of the largest skulls of any land animal ever discovered. It also had a big bony frill on its neck and a parrot-like beak at the end of its snout.

Top chewer

Triceratops had 800 teeth. When a tooth wore out from grinding and slicing the dinosaur's meals, a new one would grow in its place.

No one knows what colour Triceratops was.

Velociraptor

Velociraptor roamed the hot, dry deserts of Mongolia, China and Russia. It was only the size of a small turkey, but the bird-like dinosaur was a deadly hunter.

Hungry hunter

Velociraptor could run at high speed when it chased its prey. As well as hunting smaller dinosaurs, it feasted on the leftover bodies of animals killed by other meat-eaters.

Velociraptor was nimble and quick.

These **claws** are super-sharp!

Dangerous claws

The terrifying Velociraptor had a long curved claws on each foot, which it used to slash, stab and rip at its prey, while it held them down with its large clawed hands.

Did you know?

Fossils show that Velociraptor had feathers on its body. It laid eggs like a bird and probably made nests to protect its babies.

Stegosaurus

Stegosaurus would have been an amazing sight – it had two rows of large triangular-shaped bony plates running down its back. Even though the dinosaur had a gigantic body, its brain was the size of a walnut.

Stegosaurus grazed on grass and leaves.

Swoosh!
Swoosh!

How cool am I?

Scientists believe that Stegosaurus used its bony back plates to keep its body at the right temperature. The plates absorbed the heat of the Sun when it needed to warm up, but could also give off heat to cool it down.

Swinging spikes

Stegosaurus had two pairs of sharp spikes that stuck out from the end of its tail. If the dinosaur was attacked, it swung out its tail to deliver a deadly blow.

Scientists think that Stegosaurus' plates could change **colour**.

The end of the dinosaurs

About 65 million years ago, the dinosaurs were wiped out. Scientists have lots of different ideas why they disappeared so quickly. However, many believe the end of the dinosaurs was caused by one of two major events.

An **asteroid** zooms across the sky.

Crash landing

At this time, a giant asteroid may have smashed into the Earth. The impact would have created enough dust to block out the Sun's light. Without it, plants and animals would have died.

An explosive end

Volcanic eruptions might have caused the dinosaurs to die out. If the eruptions were powerful enough, they would have thrown rocks, gas and chemicals into the sky, poisoning the air and causing massive changes in the weather.

A **Volcano** fills the air with black smoke.

Did you know?

A huge crater made by a meteor was discovered in 1990, on the Yucatan Peninsula of Mexico, at a place called Chicxulub.

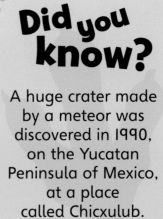

Life on Earth

We live on an incredible planet. Earth is a giant spinning ball with hot rock and liquid metal inside. The thin outside layer is called the crust. The Earth's crust is moving and changing all of the time.

Solid ground

Land, the solid part of the Earth's surface, is all around us. Whether as big as a mountain or as small as a garden, all land is made of the same things – rock, sand and soil!

Over time, rock can wear down and change shape.

Did you know?

Rock is made up of minerals, which are tiny grains of crystal or metal.

Who lives here?

The Earth's surface has many different types of habitat. A habitat is a place that contains everything a group of plants and animals need to survive. It has just the right amount of light, air, water, soil, food and shelter.

Camels are suited to a **desert** habitat.

Mountains high …

The Earth's crust is not flat – it is wrinkled! Mountains tower over valleys and plains. It takes millions of years for new mountains to appear. They are still forming all over the world.

The tops of mountains are called **peaks**.

Some caves have amazing rock formations inside.

… and caves below

Caves are underground openings in rocky sides of hills or cliffs. All caves are damp and dark. Many are deep enough to have waterfalls and lakes inside them.

Powerful plates

The Earth's crust is split into vast plates that bump and bash against each other. Sometimes hot rock and gas from deep underground manages to burst out from between the cracks.

Ready to blow

A volcano is a mountain that forms around a hole, or vent, in the ground. This hole is so deep that it connects to the hot liquid rock that is far below the Earth's surface.

The largest volcano on Earth is Mauna Loa in Hawaii.

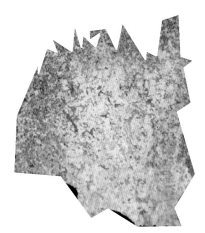

Eruption!

When enough pressure builds up, the hot liquid rock explodes through the top of the volcano. This liquid rock is called lava.

During an eruption, lava, ash and smoke spout into the air. **Whoosh!**

Liquid fire

Lava is a very hot liquid that can reach temperatures of up to 1,200 degrees Celsius! The word 'volcano' comes from the name of the Roman god of fire, Vulcan.

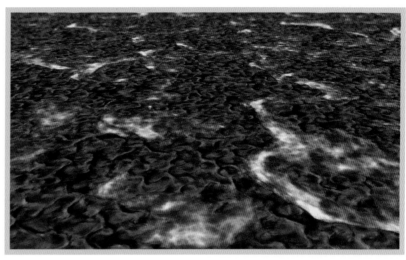

Flowing lava destroys everything in its path.

A city street after a powerful earthquake.

Crash and crack

When two of the Earth's plates knock into each other with great force, an earthquake happens. Around a million take place around the world every year. Some earthquakes make roads break up and buildings fall down.

Mind the geyser!

Sometimes liquid gets heated up deep underground. When the liquid gets too hot, jets of boiling water and steam shoot up to the surface. This is called a geyser.

Living on the land

Soil covers much of the Earth's surface. It's made from a mixture of rocks and decayed plants. Plants need soil to help them grow tall and strong and to keep their roots safe.

What grows on land?

Soil provides the nutrients and water that help plants grow. Trees, grass and flowers are all plants. A lot of the food we eat grows on the land, too. Farmers grow fruit trees, grain and vegetables.

All plants need light, water and air to help them **grow**.

In a garden, lots of different types of plants can grow together.

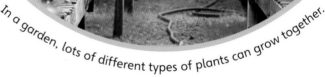

It starts with a seed!

Most plants start off as seeds. First the seed sprouts roots, which grow downwards and anchor it in the ground. After a while, a little stem pops out and grows up towards the surface.

Super sunflowers

The sunflower is one of the tallest flowers in the world. Some have grown to more than nine metres tall! Tiny seeds grow in the middle of sunflowers.

This **sunflower** is in full bloom!

This golden wheat is nearly ready to harvest.

Grasses and grains

A lot of the foods you eat, such as oats, rice and wheat, come from grasses. Even some of our sugar comes from the stem of a grass called sugar cane.

Tropical rainforest

Tropical rainforests are warm, wet forests that are home to millions of different plants and animals. Plants in rainforests create lots of the world's oxygen, which we need to breathe.

The Amazon is the world's **largest** rainforest.

Watery and wonderful

Tropical rainforests are found in Africa, Asia, Australia, India and South America. These rainforests have huge amounts of rainfall every year.

Did you know?

Trees in a tropical rainforest are so leafy and grow so close together, that rain falling on treetops can take about 10 minutes to finally reach the forest floor!

Brilliant blooms

Australian rainforests are filled with unusual flowers. Four out of every five flowers found in Australian rainforests cannot be found anywhere else on Earth.

This Australian flower is called a grevillea.

African savannah

Grasslands in Africa are called savannahs. Savannahs are covered with tall grasses that are able to grow in the sandy soil. Tough, thorny trees are the only shade for the animals that live there.

Herds of **antelopes** live on the savannah.

No rain on the plain

Although they have a rainy season that lasts several months, savannahs are hot, dry and dusty for most of the year.

Grass for grazing

Some savannah grass grows taller than you or me! Grass is an important food for animals such as zebras and antelopes. The animals spend their days grazing under the hot sun.

Australian grassland

The Australian grasslands are full of wildlife and plants, and dotted with farms, called stations. The animals living here can survive in the dry, windy weather. Emus, kangaroos, wallabies and wombats make the grasslands their home.

Sheep grazing in New South Wales, Australia.

Little mitts

Kangaroo paw is a beautiful plant found in Australia's grasslands. Its flowers look like tiny kangaroo paws! Birds called honeyeaters drink the nectar from the plant's flowers.

A tiny kangaroo paw flower.

Grrrrrr!

Dogs down under

Dingoes are wild dogs that live in Australia. They roam the grasslands in family groups called packs, which have between three and ten dogs.

Hungry dingoes hunt rodents, lizards and birds.

Desert

Deserts are the driest places on Earth. It rarely rains, so desert plants and animals – such as cactus plants and camels – must be able to survive with very little water.

This desert fox is fast asleep. **Snore!**

Staying cool

Although a few deserts are cold during the day, most are very hot and dry. During daylight, many animals escape the heat by tunnelling underground.

Many deserts are covered in **sand dunes**.

Did you know?

Africa's Sahara Desert is the largest desert in the world. It is also the hottest!

Rare rain

Rain in the desert is very rare. A storm might only happen once every few months or even years! A few weeks after it rains, wildflowers sometimes appear.

A tiny desert flower.

Watery world

Humans usually live on land, but most of the Earth is covered with oceans, rivers and lakes. Water is everywhere. People drink it, fish live in it and birds bathe in it.

Waterfalls in a forest.

Starfish only live in **saltwater**.

What is saltwater?

The water found in the ocean has lots of salt in it and is called saltwater. Lobsters, whales, dolphins, clams and starfish are just a few of the animals that live in the ocean's saltwater.

Some crocodiles live in **freshwater** rivers and lakes.

What is freshwater?

The water in lakes, ponds, rivers, streams, marshes and swamps is called freshwater. Many different fish, reptiles and amphibians live in freshwater.

Lake and pond

A lake is a large body of water surrounded by land. Some lakes are very deep. Ponds are smaller than lakes and more shallow. Lakes and ponds are home to all sorts of plants and animals.

Smooth and calm

Unlike the ocean, the water in lakes isn't constantly moving and crashing. It is actually very still. The wind, however, can create tiny waves that are called ripples.

Many woodland animals **drink** from lakes and ponds.

Did you know?

Lake Baikal in Siberia is the world's deepest and oldest lake. It is also home to the world's only freshwater seals.

Ocean

Oceans are very large bodies of water. When you go to the beach, you can see the ocean waves rolling in and out, crashing against the seashore. Ocean water is salty.

Super seas

There are five oceans in the world – the Arctic, Atlantic, Indian, Pacific and Southern. The Pacific Ocean is the biggest ocean. In fact, it covers nearly a third of the Earth's surface.

The Great Barrier Reef, the world's largest coral reef, is in the Pacific Ocean.

That's swell

Swells are stable and constant waves that have been created by storms. They can travel across entire oceans before they find land. Swells are the waves that surfers love to ride.

A surfer rides a giant **wave**.

Amazing waves

Ocean waves are caused by gusts of wind. The size and strength of waves depend on how fast the wind is blowing, where it's blowing from and how long it's been blowing.

Ocean deep

The deepest spot on Earth is the Mariana Trench in the Pacific Ocean. Even if the world's tallest mountain could sit at the bottom, its peak would be a long way below the surface!

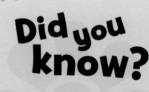

Did you know?

The ocean floor is covered with mountains, caves and valleys, just like the land.

River and stream

Rivers are wide, long bodies of flowing freshwater. Streams are shorter and narrower than rivers. Rivers and streams don't flow in a straight line, they twist and turn as they flow.

Rivers curve with the shape of the land.

On a journey

Rivers start in the mountains or hills and usually end up flowing into a large body of water, such as an ocean, bay or sea. Some rivers are muddy and brownish, while others are crystal clear.

Mega river

The Nile in Africa is the longest river in the world. It flows through 11 countries, out into the Mediterranean Sea.

Glacier and iceberg

Glaciers are like huge slow-moving rivers of ice. Icebergs are enormous chunks of ice that float in the ocean. Glaciers can be hundreds of kilometres long, while some icebergs are as big as mountains.

Break and drift

Icebergs are often found in the oceans around the North and South Pole regions, where it is very cold. They break off glaciers and ice shelves, then drift away.

Icebergs look like huge frozen mountans.

Glacial ice **crashing** into the water.

Crack, crash, snap!

When icebergs reach warmer waters, they start to melt, crack and break up. Melting ice can be very, very noisy!

Changing seasons

Our weather and temperature vary as the months pass. These changes are called seasons. Some parts of the world have two seasons a year, but others have four – spring, summer, autumn and winter.

How long is a season?

Each season is about three months long. The seasons unfold slowly, going from spring to summer to autumn to winter, then back to spring again.

Many trees change colour in the autumn.

All change!

It's not just the weather that is affected by the shifting seasons. The types of plants that bloom and the way animals behave can also change from one season to the next.

Lots of **plants** and **flowers** grow back at the same time every year.

Tropical seasons

Some parts of the world have only two seasons – dry and rainy. The lengths of the dry season and wet season can vary. The wet season is sometimes known as the monsoon season.

Some places have very **cold** winters.

Monsoon wind and rain is often very powerful.

Why do we have seasons?

The Earth takes one year to travel around the Sun. Our planet is not straight however – it is tilted to one side. So different parts of the world are closest to and get heat from the sun at different times of the year.

Did you know?

The northern and southern halves of Earth have different seasons at the same time. When it is summer in Australia, it is winter in the United Kingdom!

Spring

In some parts of the world, the weather gets warmer when spring arrives, helping to melt away winter's snow and ice. The days grow longer, which means it stays light outside later into the evening.

Spring! Spring!

Bluebells **bloom** in shady woodlands.

Bloom and grow

In spring, many flowers start blooming. Trees that have rested all winter begin growing leaves and their buds start to open. Spring often brings lots of rainy days, which are good for helping plants to grow.

Festival time

Lots of people like to celebrate the coming of spring. There are carnivals and parades all over the world. In India and Nepal, many take part in the Holi festival of colours.

Children throw coloured powder to celebrate Holi.

Busy bees

Spring is a busy time for bees.
They fly from flower to flower collecting
the nectar they need to make honey.

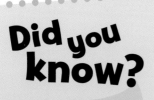

Honeybees help **flowers** and **plants** to grow.

Did you know?

Animals that sleep
during the winter, such
as bears, wake up and
look for food in the
spring. Some haven't
had anything to
eat or drink for
over 100 days!

Yawn!

Spring lambs have a soft, **woolly** coat.

Spring babies

Many animals are born in spring. Sheep living
on farms give birth to lambs, and cows
have calves. Frogs lay their eggs in ponds
and ditches, ready to grow into tadpoles.

Summer

In the northern part of the world, summer arrives around June. In the southern part, it usually starts during December. Summer is a hot and sunny time. The days grow even longer than in springtime. In some places, it stays light all through the night!

In the summer, **wildflowers** bloom in meadows and fields.

All on show

In the summer, many trees are covered with big, green leaves, providing us with shade from the Sun. Grass grows tall and the sweet smells of roses, lilies and other summer flowers often fill the air.

A bat's home is called a **roost**.

Going batty

On warm summer evenings, bats flit through the sky. They sleep all day in trees, caves or buildings, then come out at night to feed.

Many ladybirds have **spotty** bodies.

Hello, ladybird!

During the hot summer months, insects, such as ladybirds and mosquitoes, can be seen flying here and there. Ladybirds help farmers by eating up bugs that destroy their crops.

Did you know?

More thunderstorms happen during the summer than any other time of the year.

The longest day of the year

For one day in the summer, the Sun reaches its highest point in the sky. There are more hours of daylight then than on any other day of the year. It is called the summer solstice.

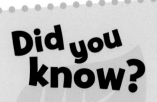

In the summer, many families go to the beach.

Autumn

In autumn, the weather gets cooler and the Sun sets earlier in the day. In some parts of the world, plants and trees change colour and animals get ready for their winter sleep.

Changing leaves

Some types of trees lose their leaves in the autumn. At first they lose their green colour, turning red, yellow and gold. As the weather gets even colder, leaves fall from the trees and turn brown and crispy.

Seek and store

When the days get shorter and it begins to get chilly outside, some animals know that it's time to start gathering nuts and berries to eat during the cold winter months.

A red squirrel **nibbles** on a nut.

All sorts of berries, nuts, fruits, vegetables and seeds appear in autumn.

Harvest time

Many delicious fruits and vegetables – such as apples, pears, pumpkins, cabbage, grapes, chestnuts, turnips and broccoli – are ready to be picked in autumn.

Time to fly

Some birds, including swallows and geese, fly away in the autumn. They make incredible journeys to faraway places where the weather is warmer. They return again in the spring.

Geese can fly great distances.

Winter

By the time winter arrives in some parts of the world, autumn's colourful leaves have gone and the trees are bare. During this season, frost often appears on plants in the morning.

A **winter** sunset over a frozen lake..

Short and dark
Winter days are very short. The Sun sets early in the evening and, without its light to warm the air, the temperature gets colder. The shortest day of winter is called the winter solstice.

The big freeze
In many places, winter is the coldest time of the year. It can get very windy and snowy outside. Ponds and lakes may freeze and turn to ice.

Winter weasel

Some animals change their appearance in winter. The weasel's brown coat turns white. This helps it to blend in with snow and stay hidden from enemies. In spring, the weasel will shed its white coat and grow a brown one again.

A weasel's coat can change when winter arrives.

The holly tree has **scarlet** berries.

Test of time

Some trees keep their leaves and berries all through the winter. They are called evergreens. The oldest living tree is an evergreen. One American bristlecone pine is around 5,000 years old!

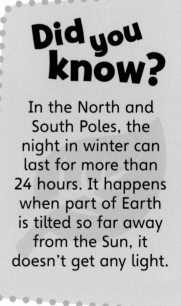

Did you know?

In the North and South Poles, the night in winter can last for more than 24 hours. It happens when part of Earth is tilted so far away from the Sun, it doesn't get any light.

Changing skies

When we talk about weather, we're talking about what the air is like in a certain place. Does it feel hot and dry when you step outside? Is it cold, damp or windy? Weather happens in the layer of air around the Earth called the atmosphere.

What is weather?

Weather is made up of different things, such as wind, temperature, sunshine and clouds. Weather is always changing. It changes from hour to hour and day to day.

It can even **rain** on sunny days!

Measuring weather

Weather stations use special instruments to measure changes in the weather. Computers record rainfall, the temperature and the speed that the wind is blowing. There are weather stations all over the world.

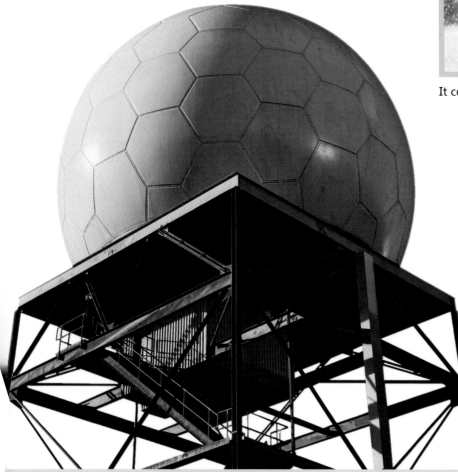

Weather stations can be on dry land or out at sea.

Eyes in the sky

Machines called satellites travel around the Earth, taking pictures and gathering detailed information about the weather. They can pick up changes that are difficult to see down on the ground.

A weather satellite picture of the Earth.

Fog surrounds the tall Golden Gate bridge in America.

Did you know?

Water in the air affects the weather. Without water, there could be no clouds, rain, lightning or snow!

What is the weather today?

People who study the weather are called meteorologists. They use the information from weather stations and satellites to work out what the weather will be like in the days and weeks ahead.

Swoosh!

Clouds

Clouds are formed from water in the air that you can't see. This 'invisible water' is called water vapour. When water vapour rises high into the sky, where it is very cold, the vapour forms a cloud.

Cumulus clouds are often low in the sky.

Did you know?

Clouds are white because they reflect the light from the Sun. Some clouds float near to the ground, others are very high in the sky.

Cirrus clouds are shaped by strong winds.

Stratus clouds cover the sky like a blanket.

Seeing shapes

Some clouds look like big puffs of cotton wool. These are called cumulus clouds. There are other types of clouds, too. Cirrus clouds are thin and curly, while stratus clouds look like long, flat layers of white.

Rain clouds

Dark grey clouds are called nimbus clouds. When you see nimbus clouds filling the sky and making it dark, it means that it's going to rain.

Grey **nimbus** clouds gather over a valley.

Thunderclouds have water droplets at the bottom and ice crystals at the top.

Stormy skies

A cumulonimbus cloud is a large, dark and puffy cloud that's electrically charged. Cumulonimbus clouds are better known as thunderclouds!

Flying high

Sometimes when aeroplanes jet through the air, they leave a long trail of clouds behind them. These are called contrails. Contrails look like puffy white lines, criss-crossing the sky.

Rain

Rain happens when the vapour that forms clouds turns into droplets of water. The droplets get bigger and bigger, until they are too heavy to float in the air. Then they fall from the sky in a rain shower.

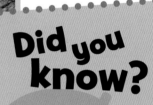

Did you know?

As raindrops fall they hit other raindrops and change size. Each one looks like a flattened jellybean.

Umbrellas keep us dry when it is raining.

Drizzle or downpour?

Raindrops can come down in a gentle sprinkle, or in heavy sheets that sometimes cause leaves and flowers to break off from their stems.

74

Drink up!

Rain soaks into the ground, giving trees, grass, flowers, fruits and vegetables the water they need to grow.

Spring flowers in the rain.

Water works

Some rain seeps deep into the earth. Humans use wells and underground pipes to bring that rainwater up out of the ground. The water has to be treated before it can be used for washing and drinking.

Rainbows appear in the sky, **opposite** the Sun.

I can see a rainbow

Sometimes when there is sun and rain at the same time, a rainbow appears. Beams of sunlight separate into seven bright colours as they shine through the raindrops. This creates a giant arch in the sky.

Thunder and lightning

There are millions of water droplets in rain clouds. During a storm, the droplets rub against each other, creating electricity. This is called lightning! Thunder is the noise that a lightning strike makes.

Lightning **striking** the ground.

Rumbly thunder

The temperature of a lightning bolt is hotter than the Sun. Since lightning heats the air so quickly, a bolt makes the cold air around it shake with a loud sound, called thunder.

Did you know?

In a storm, we see lightning before we hear the thunder. This is because light travels faster than sound.

Storm central

Every second of every day, there are around 100 instances of lightning striking the ground somewhere in the world!

Bolts from the blue

Lightning can look like
a set of jagged lines
cracking up the sky.
This is the electricity from
rain clouds jumping down
towards the ground.

Cr..k!

Lightning is a **spectacular** sight.

A lightning strike lasts for a split second, but it is very powerful.

Near or far?

If you listen closely to
the sound of thunder,
you can tell how close
the lightning is. If it's far
away, you may hear
a low rumble or no sound
at all. The closer that the
lightning gets, the louder
the crackle or bang
it makes.

Snow

In cold temperatures, clouds will form ice crystals instead of raindrops. After a while, the crystals start to stick together. When they become too heavy to stay in the air, the crystals fall to the ground as snow.

Igloos have a dome-shaped roof and a small doorway to keep in the heat.

Out of the cold

In the Arctic, people on hunting trips may build shelters made of snow. These shelters are called igloos. Even though they're made using big blocks of snow, igloos help people to stay warm by keeping hot air trapped inside and the cold air outside.

Shapes and sides

All snowflakes have six sides, but no two snowflakes look exactly alike. When it's very cold, snowflakes are small, long and thin. When it's slightly warmer, they're larger and have more detailed shapes.

Tiny crystals

Snowflakes begin as ice crystals
that are as small as specks of dust.
As they fall, the crystals connect to
other crystals and form snowflakes.
Some snowflakes look like flowers,
stars, spiderwebs or even lightning bolts.

It is easy to make a **snow angel.**

A skier **jumps** *above the snow.*

Snowy sports

Some sports rely on snowfall every winter.
Skiing, snowboarding and ski jumping all
need snowy conditions. Special machines
flatten the snow on mountains so that
athletes can compete.

Wind

Although you can't see the wind, you can feel it moving. Sometimes it can be very powerful, making kites and leaves – or even hundreds of balloons – lift into the air. At other times the wind can feel like a soft whisper against your skin.

Wind power

Sometimes we use the wind's energy to make machines and vehicles move. Windmills are farm machines that use the wind's energy to pump water or grind up grain.

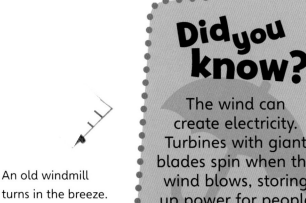

An old windmill turns in the breeze.

Did you know?

The wind can create electricity. Turbines with giant blades spin when the wind blows, storing up power for people to use in their homes.

Nature's gardener

The wind carries plant seeds from one place to another. Wherever the seeds fall, they have a chance to grow into new plants. Many flowers and plants have grown from seeds that were blown in from far away.

Dandelion seeds get **scattered** by the wind.

A **kitesurfer** uses the wind to pull her across the water.

Blowing along

Some people use the wind to do fun water sports, like kitesurfing! A popular kitesurfing place is the southern coast of Spain. A thin stretch of water called the Strait of Gibraltar forms a perfect wind tunnel between Spain and Africa.

How strong?

Wind can blow at different strengths. A light wind is called a breeze, but if the air moves more quickly it can become a gale. Hurricanes bring super-strong winds that have the power to destroy buildings and tear up trees.

Sometimes hurricanes can cause **damage** to houses.

Where we live

The world is divided into huge areas called continents. There are people meeting, working, playing and going about their daily lives on every continent, even icy Antarctica. Inside most of the continents, there are many countries.

The world's **biggest** country is Russia. Moscow is the capital.

Great and small

There are seven continents. The biggest by land area is Asia. The smallest is Oceania – it includes the countries of Australia, New Zealand and thousands of tiny Pacific Islands.

A view over St Peter's Square in Vatican City.

Did you know?

Vatican City is the world's smallest country. The tiny nation sits within an area of Rome, Italy's capital city. It is about the same size as a golf course!

Melting middle

There is an imaginary line running around the middle of the Earth called the Equator, which is between the North and South Poles. The hottest countries of the world are the ones closest to the Equator.

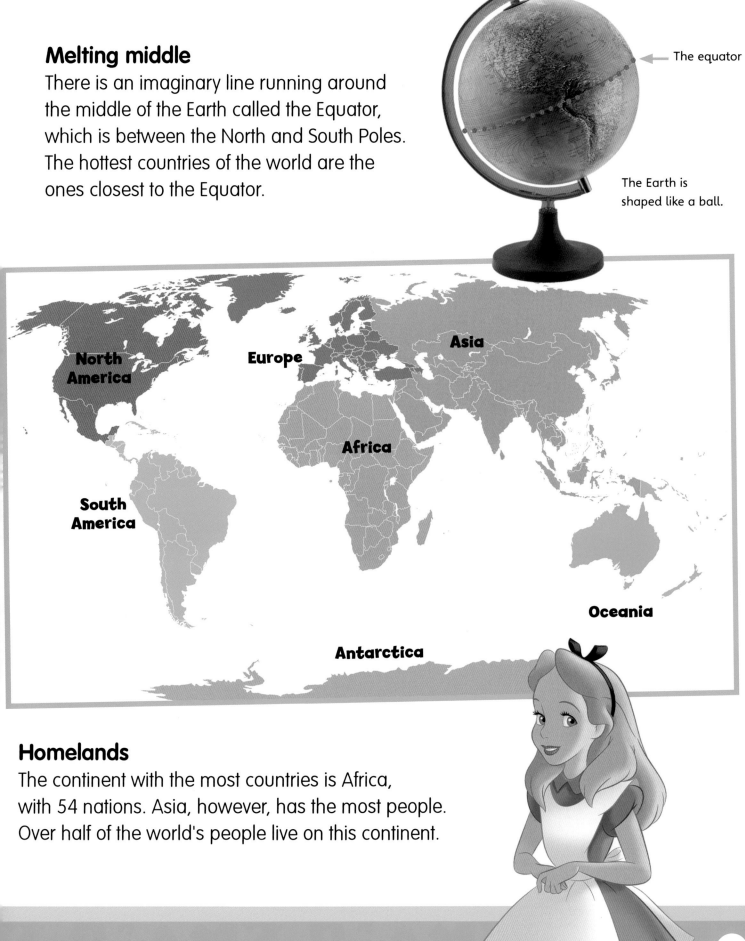

The equator

The Earth is shaped like a ball.

North America

Europe

Asia

Africa

South America

Oceania

Antarctica

Homelands

The continent with the most countries is Africa, with 54 nations. Asia, however, has the most people. Over half of the world's people live on this continent.

People of the world

There are more than seven billion of us living in the world. In different places, people have different thoughts, feelings, ideas and beliefs. When you travel the world you can see that people live their lives in lots of different ways.

City streets bustle with busy people.

Look at me!
The world is full of people, but everyone looks different. We have different shaped bodies and different coloured hair, skin and eyes.

Hello, hello!
Language is spoken and written words. This is how we communicate with each other. There are over 6,500 languages spoken around the world!

Bonjour!
French

Hujambo!
Swahili

Hello!
English

Traditions and customs

Every country has its own traditions and customs – from the way that people dress, to the food they eat, the houses they live in, the things they celebrate and the laws that govern their lands. People like to relax in different ways, too.

These children live in East Africa.

Back to basics

Despite our differences, we all need the same basic things to lead a happy, healthy life. All people need water to drink and food to eat. We need a place to shelter, and our families and friends.

Hola!
Spanish

Namaste!
Hindi

Marhaba!
Arabic

Ni hao!
Mandarin

Homes

Our houses are our homes. They are the places where we live, eat and sleep. There are many different types of home. Depending on where you live in the world, your home could be a house, a tent, a boat, a caravan or a hut.

Building blocks

People usually make their houses from the materials found in the area they live in. Houses can be made from brick, stone, wood, mud, grass, blocks of snow or even animal skins and hair.

Keeping comfy

In cold countries, our houses need to keep us warm so we build them from materials that keep the heat in. In hot countries, houses are built so they stay cool inside. They might have shutters on the windows to keep the Sun out.

Some houses are built on **stilts** to keep them dry and above water.

Cities and towns

A city is a large place where people come to live, work and study. In cities, there are museums, art galleries, theatres and famous monuments to visit, as well as restaurants, parks and shops.

A small town in England.

Tokyo, in Japan, is one of the **busiest** cities in the world.

City or town?

A town is like a city, just smaller and less busy, and fewer people live there. Many towns have weekly markets, where local people sell and buy goods like food, clothes and things for the home.

City life

Cities are busy places full of houses and buildings of all shapes and sizes, such as offices, apartments, schools and hospitals. The streets are packed with people, buses and cars.

Did you know?

In the past, most people used to live in the countryside. Now, over half the world's population lives in a city or a town.

Jobs and work

We need money to buy food and clothes, to keep our homes comfortable and to travel to different places. People work to earn money to do all of these things. Some people work on their own and others work in a team.

What will you be?

When you grow up and finish school, you will be able to get a job. You might want to be a pilot or a scientist, a chef or a designer, a vet or a mechanic. The choice is yours!

Vets work with all types of **animals**.

Tools of the trade

Whatever job you do, you will probably have to study and learn how to do it. You might work in an office or a factory, on a farm or in a film studio. You might use computers or work with special tools.

Sparks are hot! Welders wear thick gloves and heavy helmets.

Teachers help students to learn new things.

Hard hats and neon jackets keep people **safe** while they are working.

What to wear?

People wear special clothes for certain jobs. If you are a police officer or a soldier, you wear a uniform. If you are a surgeon in a hospital, you wear a gown, cap and mask. If you work on a building site, you wear a hard hat and boots.

Food

We all need food to live and grow. The meals we eat come from plants and animals. There is an amazing variety! People eat different foods and cook in different ways, depending on where they live in the world.

These women are picking tea leaves.

Plants to eat

Vegetables, fruits and grains all are types of food plants. Eating them keeps us healthy. And they taste good! Rice, wheat, maize and potatoes make up the basic diet for everyone around the world.

Cows provide meat and dairy foods.

Meat, milk and more

Animals like chickens, pigs, sheep and cows are farmed for their meat. We also eat other products that come from animals like milk, eggs and honey.

Food from home

Each part of the world has its own special dishes. All over the globe, people make and share food to celebrate their festivals, customs and traditions.

Did you know?

Carrots were originally white, red, yellow or purple! Orange carrots were specially bred from mixing the red and yellow varieties.

You need two **chopsticks** to pick up food.

Pizza comes from Italy.

Table manners

In some countries people eat their food with wooden sticks called chopsticks. In others they use a knife and a fork, and elsewhere people use their hands.

Clothes and fashion

We wear clothes to keep us warm in cold climates, cool in hot climates, and to protect us from the weather, like rain or snow. We also wear clothes that reflect the traditions of the country we live in and the way of life there.

Weave and stitch

Clothes are made from many different materials. Some of these are natural. They come from an animal or a plant, like animal skins, wool, silk and cotton. Other materials, like nylon and plastic, are man-made.

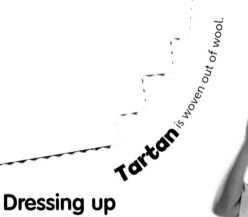

Tartan is woven out of wool.

Dressing up

Special clothes are worn for certain jobs or for important occasions. Many children wear uniforms for school or special clothes for their hobbies. This might be a football kit, a dance outfit or a scout uniform.

Fantastic fashion

Fashion designers put on shows to display their latest collection of outfits. The looks and trends change all the time, so what looks cool now might be old-fashioned next year!

Fashion models walk along a stage called a **catwalk**.

Children in Peru wear brightly coloured hats and ponchos.

Did you know?

In India, it is traditional for women to wear a robe called a sari. The sari is made from a single piece of cloth, but it can be wrapped around the body in lots of different ways.

National costume

Most countries have a national costume. This is an outfit that reflects the traditions and history of a country. It often uses materials, colours, decorations and styles that have been around for a very long time.

Sport

There are all sorts of sports to enjoy – from football and athletics, to swimming, golf and cycling. They can be played in a team or by just one person, as a job or just for fun. Sport is a good way to keep fit and healthy.

Football

Football is the most popular sport on the planet. National teams enter big competitions and attract famous players, as well as millions of fans from every part of the globe.

Many children play **football** every weekend in their local park.

We are the champions!

Sporting events and competitions take place all over the world. Some events are held in enormous arenas that seat thousands of people. Others take place in local parks, fields and halls.

Ice hockey is played with a stick and a puck.

Kit list

Some sports need special equipment. A player might need a snowboard, water skis or even a motorcycle in order to take part! Other sportsmen and women, like runners, just need the right pair of shoes.

The Olympic Games

The modern Olympic Games is a huge festival of sport and athletics. There are winter and summer competitions. Sportsmen and women try to win medals and break sporting records.

Visitors going to see the summer Olympic Games in London 2012.

The arts

Art is a creative activity, such as painting, sculpting, acting, dancing, writing or music. Artists and performers use their skills to express their feelings and tell stories. Art, in any form, can be anything that you imagine!

Photography is a form of art.

Acting and dancing

Actors and dancers use their skills to entertain us or to celebrate an occasion, whether it is for a performance at a festival or the theatre, or recorded for a movie. There are many styles of acting and dancing.

Dancers must be graceful and fit.

Painting and sculpting

There are lots of ways of making art. Artists use different materials like paint, wood, clay or metal. Pictures or sculptures can be based on real life or just made up of shapes, patterns and colours. Every artist has his or her own style.

A tale to tell

We use words to communicate with each other. Writers tell stories, give us information and express their feelings with words. We can enjoy this form of art by reading books, poems and newspapers.

This girl is learning the **violin**.

Magical music

All around the world, people make music with instruments or just by singing, clapping or stamping their feet! Jazz, pop and folk are all different types of music, but there are many more.

A **sitar** is a traditional Indian instrument.

Boom! Boom!

Moving around

Transport allows people and goods to move from one place to another. It has changed how people work and live. Before transport, people couldn't go far, as they had to walk or ride on animals. Now they can explore the whole world!

Ways to go

There are many ways to travel by land, sea or air. Cars, trains, boats and aeroplanes are all types of transport, called vehicles, that help carry people to where they want to go.

By land

We need roads and train tracks to travel over land. We can go long or short distances, but cars, buses and trains can be noisy and pollute the air.

Cars and buses drive along roads, but trains travel on tracks.

By air

We can travel long distances through the sky, and visit other countries anywhere in the world. Air travel is the fastest way to get around, but it is also the most expensive.

People use ferries to travel across water.

By water

We can also voyage long distances by sea or other waterways like rivers and canals. Travelling by boat or ship is not as fast as travelling by aeroplane, however.

Transport network

To get from one place to another we need a system of special places where we can start and finish our journeys – airports, bus and train stations, ports and roads.

Did you know?

The invention of the wheel close to 6,000 years ago changed the way in which humans got around. People could suddenly be rolled and pulled along at much faster speeds.

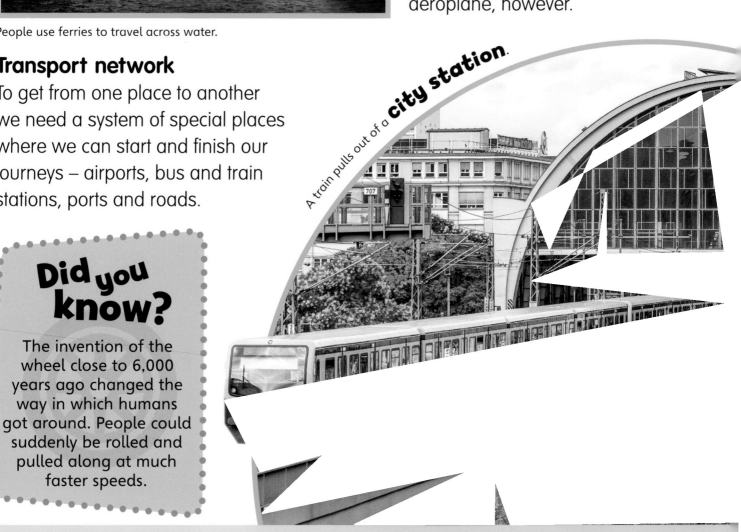

A train pulls out of a city station.

Cars and trucks

There are all sorts of types, sizes and models of cars. Cars usually have four wheels and an engine, which uses fuel, to make them go. Some trucks are massive machines, hauling heavy loads along our roads and motorways.

This mighty **truck** is being used in Australia.

An **ambulance** is an emergency vehicle.

Working wheels

At first cars were made to get people from place to place. Later they were designed to do jobs. Fire engines and police cars rush to emergencies, while vans and lorries transport food and heavy materials.

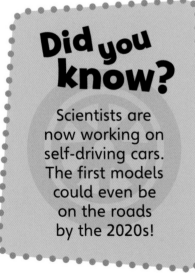

Did you know?

Scientists are now working on self-driving cars. The first models could even be on the roads by the 2020s!

Shiny and sporty

People use cars to get them to work, to school, to the shops or to visit their friends. There are also fast, luxury cars for people who want to be noticed, and even faster cars for racing around tracks at sporting events.

Vroom! Vroom!

Bicycles and motorbikes

A bicycle can have two or three wheels. It is the most common form of transport in the world! A motorbike has wheels like a bicycle, but it also has an engine and needs fuel like a car. Motorbikes can drive at high speeds.

Children riding on **mountain bikes**.

Green and clean

A bicycle doesn't use fuel, so it doesn't cause any pollution. It is great for travelling short distances and for having fun. Cycling is also a popular racing sport.

Motorbikes **tilt** as they turn.

Speedy vehicles

Motorbike riders have to wear a helmet, special thick trousers and a jacket to protect them in case they fall off. Motorbikes are used in racing. It takes a lot of skill to drive fast around a track and balance on two wheels.

Air travel

The quickest way to travel is by jet aeroplane. Jets can travel at incredible speeds, but there are other ways to fly. Helicopters, gliders and hot-air balloons all travel through the air.

Hot-air balloons **float** in the sky.

Flying without wings

A helicopter has rotor blades at the top that spin very fast. It can fly in any direction and hover on the spot. Two smaller blades at the back stop it from wobbling.

Lift off!

Aeroplanes are built with specially shaped bodies and wings that help them fly. Their powerful engine drives them forward very quickly. This forces air to rush over and under the nose and wings of the plane, lifting it up into the air.

A passenger aeroplane takes off.

Did you know?

There are lots of different types of aircraft, from single-seaters to large jumbo jets that can carry over 800 passengers!

Trains and buses

Trains are built to transport people or loads along tracks. Some heavy goods trains can pull hundreds of carriages and wagons behind them! Buses are large passenger vehicles that travel along the road.

A modern double-decker bus.

Transport for all

City buses travel along fixed routes. Many buses have two decks to sit on. Others have a stretchy section in the middle so that they can bend around curves in the road.

Rail racers

Trains can go very fast and they don't get stuck in traffic jams like cars. The first trains were powered by coal and steam engines, but now modern trains run on electricity, diesel or even magnets.

Japanese **bullet trains** can travel at high speed.

Boats and ships

There are all sorts of ways to get around on the water – from small canoes to yachts, motorboats and vast container ships. Boats are used to carry people and goods around the world, for fishing, for sports or just for fun.

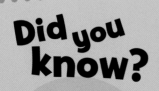

Did you know?

The main body of a boat is called the hull. The front is called the bow and the back is called the stern.

Power up

Boats need power to move through the water. Some, like rowing boats, are people-powered. Others use sails and the force of the wind to push them forward. Speedboats and large ships use engines and fuel.

A **speedboat** is able to race through calm waters.

Submarines

A submarine is a special vessel that can go underwater. It can explore the depths of the seas and oceans where divers cannot reach. Submarines are also used to help recover ships that have sunk, or to protect countries around the world.

Sink and surface

A submarine has special tanks called ballasts that help it sink below the waves. The tanks are filled with water, making the submarine heavier. To come back up, the water is pumped out of the tanks into the sea.

A submarine can stay **underwater** for months.

The cockpit of a modern submarine.

Safe and sound

Submarines use sonar equipment to help them find their way through the dark oceans. A sound wave is sent out. When it hits an object it sends back a signal, so that the submarine knows where to go without bumping into anything.

Amazing me!

Your body is an astonishing, living machine. It is made up of many different parts – skin, organs, bones, muscles, blood and nerves, which all have special jobs to do. The human body is incredibly complicated, yet most of it is made up of water.

Brand-new you

A new life begins with one tiny cell. That cell will multiply countless times, as a human being slowly forms and develops. Every baby that is born shares some of the same features as their mother and father.

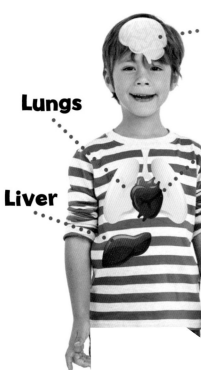

Brain

Heart

Lungs

Liver

Babies **learn** and **grow** very quickly.

Working hard

Organs are important parts of the body. The brain sends signals to all of the other organs to make them work. Each one does something unique. The lungs breathe in air. The heart pumps the blood around your body. The liver cleans the blood.

Bony bodies

Inside every body there is a skeleton, a strong framework that enables it to stay upright and keep its shape. The skeleton is made up of 206 bones. The bones help you move and protect your organs, too.

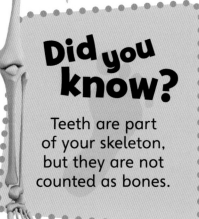

The bones that make up our skeletons are hard on the outside.

Did you know?

Teeth are part of your skeleton, but they are not counted as bones.

Bones help us to **jump**, run and kick.

All wrapped up

Your skin is the largest organ that you have! There's a thin layer of it all over you, from the top of your head to the tips of your fingers. Skin protects you from germs and stops your body from getting too hot or too cold.

Move a muscle

Muscles help you to move your body – you have more than 640 of them! Some help you to run and walk, others help you to stretch, jump, blink and breathe. Muscles are joined to the bones by tendons.

Heart and blood

The heart is a special muscle that pumps the blood all around the body, so that it can deliver oxygen and food to every part, and take away any waste. The blood travels through a system of thin tubes called blood vessels.

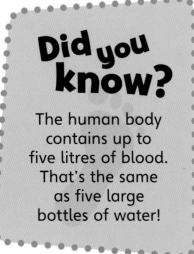

Did you know?

The human body contains up to five litres of blood. That's the same as five large bottles of water!

What is blood?

Blood is made up of cells. Red blood cells carry oxygen. White blood cells keep the blood clean and fight germs. Others called platelets help you to heal if you cut yourself.

Blood flows through tubes called **blood vessels**.

Powerful pump

The heart is made up of two sack-like pumps that squeeze blood around the body all through your life. The blood leaves the heart through blood vessels called arteries and returns to the heart through blood vessels called veins.

Your heart beats between 70 and 100 times a minute.

The lungs

The oxygen in the air helps us get energy from the foods that we eat. We could not live without it. Our lungs allow us to breathe in air and transport the oxygen into our blood system.

Running uses up lots of air, so we have to **breathe** more quickly.

How we breathe

We have a special muscle called the diaphragm and muscles in the ribs to help us breathe. Air comes in through the nose, then travels down our windpipe towards the lungs.

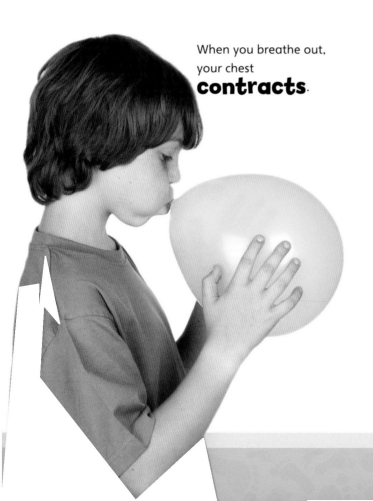

When you breathe out, your chest **contracts**.

In and out

When we breathe in, the diaphragm flattens out and the lungs get bigger. The ribs lift outwards to give the lungs more space. When we breathe out, the diaphragm pushes up and the ribs pull back in, and the lungs get smaller.

The brain

The brain is like a computer that controls our body functions, what we do, how we move and what we think. It also stores our memories. The brain contains billions of nerve cells that receive and send information to the rest of the body.

Five fantastic senses

Our senses tell our bodies what is happening around us. Each one takes the information it receives and sends signals back to the brain. The brain processes the signals so we understand what we are seeing, hearing, smelling, tasting or touching.

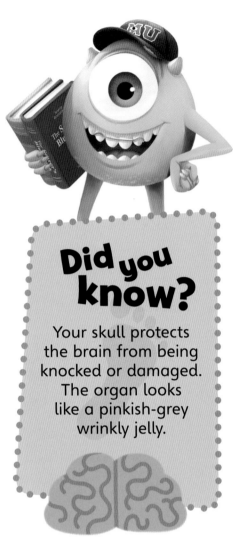

Did you know?

Your skull protects the brain from being knocked or damaged. The organ looks like a pinkish-grey wrinkly jelly.

See

Touch

Taste

Hear

Smell

A complex machine

Each part of the brain has its own special job to do. One area concentrates on what you are feeling, while others focus on different things such as solving problems and understanding speech.

Eating

Our bodies break down the food we eat, turning it into chemicals that give us the energy we need to live. Imagine a long tube that starts at the mouth, then goes down through the stomach to the intestines.

This girl is eating a watermelon.

The journey begins

When we put food into our mouth, it gets broken down into small pieces by the teeth and mixed with saliva (spit), which makes it easier to swallow. It then travels down a tube to the stomach.

Taking what we need

Food is squeezed in the stomach and mixed with special juices. It moves to the small intestine where all the useful chemicals are absorbed. This is called digestion. The chemicals are sent to the liver and then passed on to the rest of the body.

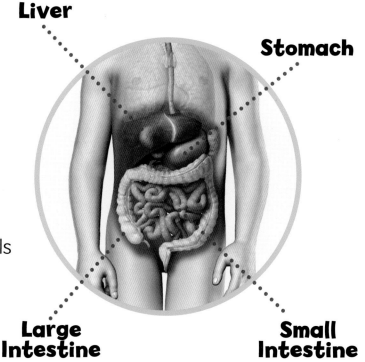

Liver

Stomach

Large Intestine

Small Intestine

A healthy life

The body needs to be looked after to keep it healthy and working properly. Eating the right kinds of food, exercising, keeping clean and getting enough sleep are all good ways to keep your body working well, and to make you feel happy.

A balanced diet

To stay healthy, we need to eat a range of foods. A balanced diet is made up of a mixture of food from all of these groups.

Did you know?

Fats and sugars give you lots of energy, but they don't contain many good nutrients, so you shouldn't eat too much of anything in this group.

Fruit and vegetables

Fats and sugars

Dairy

Protein   **Carbohydrates**

Wonderful water

Our bodies need lots of water! We should drink at least five glasses every single day. Water helps to keep you cool, protect your organs, and carry chemicals and oxygen around your body.

We all need water to live.

Keeping fit

Exercise makes you feel good and keeps your body healthy. There are lots of fun ways you can keep fit, from going for a walk, riding a bicycle, swimming, playing football or just running around your local park.

Sleeping well is an important part of being **healthy**.

Night, night!

While you sleep your body grows and repairs itself, so it's important to get enough every night. Sleep also allows your body to rest so that you have lots of energy to work and play in the daytime.

World of wonder

Science helps us understand everything around us. We use it to find out how things work or why they happen the way they do. Technology uses science to invent new things that might help us in our daily lives, like computers, vehicles or medicine.

Let's experiment!

People that study science are called scientists. They try to find out how the world works and solve big problems by asking questions, studying objects closely and carrying out tests called experiments.

These children are doing a **chemistry** experiment.

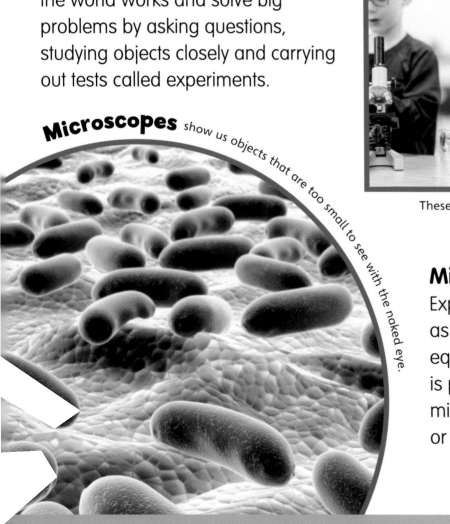

Microscopes show us objects that are too small to see with the naked eye.

Mixed results

Experiments don't always turn out as scientists expect. Sometimes the equipment doesn't work or an idea is proved to be wrong. The results might even solve a different question or reveal something unexpected.

Scientists working in a lab.

Testing and measuring

Some scientists work outside, and others work in offices. Many set up experiments in a special room called a laboratory. A laboratory (lab) has all the equipment that a scientist needs, such as test tubes, computers and microscopes.

All sorts of science

There are many different kinds of science. Physics is the study of matter and energy – light, heat, motion, sound and electricity. Chemistry is the study of the elements and chemicals that make up our world. Biology is the study of living things.

Geology is the study of rocks and the Earth.

Botany is the study of plants.

Did you know?

Scientists have worked out that everything on Earth is made of tiny particles called atoms. There are over 100 different kinds.

Famous scientists

Scientists have been searching for knowledge for thousands of years. Many have helped us to understand more about our world. These scientists will always be remembered for making all of our lives better and easier.

Galileo Galilei

Galileo was an Italian scientist who lived over 400 years ago. He studied physics and astronomy. He invented the world's first telescope, which he used to look at the surface of the Moon.

Astronomy is the study of space.

Gravity makes these leaves fall to the ground.

Albert Einstein

Some say that Einstein was the greatest scientist of all. He was born in Germany in 1879. His work shaped our ideas about how the Universe works. Einstein came up with a famous theory that helped explain gravity and energy.

Charles Darwin

A statue of Charles Darwin.

Darwin was an English scientist who studied nature. He believed that animals change over time to form new species. He called this evolution. Darwin's work changed the way people understood their own existence in the world.

Marie Curie

Sometimes scientists make discoveries that save lives. Marie Curie was a Polish physicist who studied radioactivity. She trained nurses how to take images of the insides of the body using X-rays.

The **Internet** helps us to learn new things.

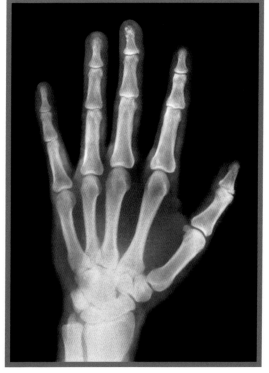

This X-ray shows the bones inside a hand.

Tim Berners-Lee

This English scientist invented the World Wide Web. It allows pages on the Internet to be linked together. This led to the creation of a massive library of information that people from all around the globe can read on their computers.

Great inventions

Some of the earliest inventions were probably not thought up by one single person. Instead they were developed and improved over time. As our knowledge of the world grows, so we are able to invent more and more useful things.

A heavy stone **wheel**.

First things first

Early men and women discovered how to make tools and weapons out of stone and then metal. They learned how to use fire to cook and keep them warm, make clothes and tents out of animal skins and how to move heavy loads with wheels.

Stargazing

The Chinese were the first people to develop a compass, but early sailors worked out that the stars could help them to find their way. This meant that they could sail their boats without getting lost, even when they couldn't see land.

Early sailors used certain stars as guide points.

This **sun dial** has been marked with the hours of the day.

What's the time?

Clocks and watches come in all shapes and sizes now, but the earliest clocks were simple sticks stuck into the ground. People could tell what time of day it was by the length and position of the shadow cast by the stick.

Lightbulb moment

Up until the late 1800s, people still had to read in the evenings by fire or candlelight. American scientist Thomas Edison changed all that. He came up with the electric lightbulb, and a network to light up homes all across a city.

The **bright lights** of a busy city.

Did you know?

The famous artist Leonardo da Vinci was also an inventor. He drew plans for a helicopter and a diving suit, hundreds of years before anyone else thought of them.

Communication

We communicate with each other by talking or writing, by drawing pictures, signs or symbols, or by making sounds or movements. Modern technology allows us to communicate quickly and easily using our phones and computers.

Egyptian hieroglyphics.

Ancient messages

The first written types of communication were drawings or marks and symbols, which showed details about people's daily lives. The ancient Egyptians used pictures called hieroglyphs to tell their stories.

Spread the word

Johannes Gutenberg, who was a German blacksmith, invented the first printing press. The press allowed books to be printed and owned by more people. It also helped the sharing of information and ideas around the world.

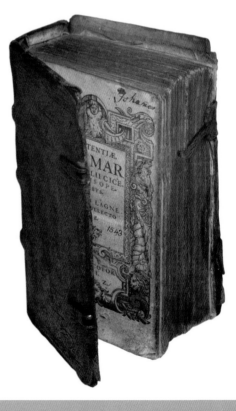

Communicating today

Nowadays people send e-mails, texts or share messages online to talk about what they are doing or thinking. They can even add little picture symbols called smileys or emoticons to show how they are feeling!

A **happy** emoticon.

It's fun to communicate with our friends.

Ships use **flags** to communicate at sea.

Give me a sign

There are lots of ways to communicate without speaking or writing. Semaphore is a way of holding up flags to pass on messages. Morse code uses flashes of light or beeping sounds. Puffs of smoke from a fire can be used to make a signal.

Making connections

If we want to find out about the world around us we can watch television or read a newspaper or book. Even if someone lives on the other side of the world, we can communicate with them via the Internet or telephone.

Robots

Robots are machines that work on their own to do specific jobs. They have computers inside them that are programmed to tell them what to do. Robots come in all shapes and sizes. Some are even made to look like people or animals!

Robots working in a car factory.

Factory workers

Robots are used in factories to make all sorts of things, from cars and phones to food products. They can work without a break, unlike people, and they can do jobs that are too difficult or dangerous for people to do.

Danger zones

Robots can be used to rescue people from collapsed buildings after an earthquake, without risking other human lives. They can even be used to do research near volcanoes, deep underwater or in places that are difficult to get to.

A modern **Police** robot.

This robotic craft is on a mission to Saturn.

Space robots

Special robot machines are used to explore planets in space because it is too dangerous to send astronauts to such remote places. The robots collect information and take pictures to help scientists with their research.

Did you know?

Surgeons use special robots to help them perform difficult operations.

The future

Scientists are busy working on new robots that will be able to make decisions and solve problems by themselves. In the future, robots might be able to help us with more of our daily jobs.

There are already robots, like this one, that can do the **Vacuuming**!

Our Universe

The Sun, Moon and stars are very far away from us. Everything that exists beyond the Earth's atmosphere is called space. Exploring space is very difficult as there is no air to breathe and the distances between things are huge.

What are planets?

Very far away, high up in the sky are big, round objects called planets. There are eight planets in our Solar System, including Earth. Some are mostly made of gas, but others are made of rock and metal.

Saturn is the second largest planet.

The Sun **rising** over the Earth.

What is a star?

A star is a massive ball of burning gas. The nearest star to Earth is the Sun. We can see many other stars from our planet, but they are much further away. The hot gas in each star burns so fiercely it creates light that shines in the night sky.

What else is up in space?

Space contains many billions of galaxies. These are collections of stars, planets and dust. Our Solar System is found in a galaxy called the Milky Way.

This is the Milky Way.

How do we learn about space?

Scientists who study space are called astronomers. They use powerful telescopes to help them see distant planets and stars. The Hubble Space Telescope floats above the Earth, observing objects in space.

Earth is the third planet from the Sun.

Did you know?

Space is completely silent. Without air, it is impossible for sound to travel from one place to another.

Solar System

The Sun is the centre of the Earth's solar system. 'Solar' means belonging to the Sun. Our Solar System includes all of the objects that move around it. The planets and their moons, gas, rock and space dust orbit this giant star.

A family of planets

Earth, the planet we live on, is one of eight planets that travel around the Sun.

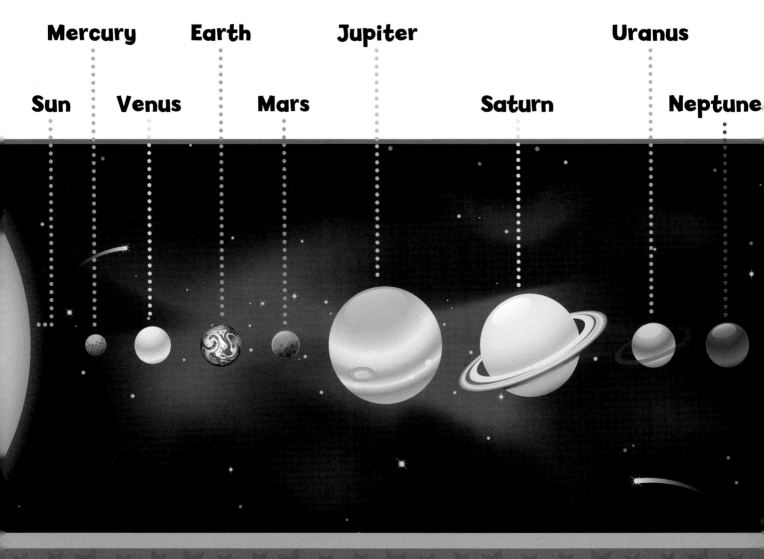

Mercury   Earth   Jupiter   Uranus

Sun   Venus   Mars   Saturn   Neptune

In a spin

Each planet in the Solar System takes a different amount of time to circle around the Sun. It takes one year for the Earth to travel around the Sun once, with most years lasting 365 days.

Sometimes asteroids **crash** into other planets.

The Sun gives us heat and light on Earth.

Flying rocks

What else would you find floating around our Solar System? Millions of asteroids! They are pieces of rock left over from the formation of the Solar System nearly 4.6 billion years ago.

Glittering comets

A comet is a ball of rock, snow and ice. When it gets close to the Sun, the ice in it begins to melt. The melting ice, gas and dust in the comet combine to create a bright tail that glows behind it.

A comet blazes across the sky.

Did you know?

The Solar System also has smaller objects inside it called dwarf planets. Most are made of ice. The largest dwarf planet is Pluto. It was only discovered in 1930.

Earth

We all live on the planet called Earth. It is the only planet in the Solar System that we know of with people, plants and animals living on it. Earth is just the right distance from the Sun, so it is heated to the perfect temperature for us to survive.

Merry-go-round

Although you can't feel it, the Earth is constantly spinning. The side of the planet that faces the Sun changes as it turns. It takes 24 hours – one whole day – for the Earth to spin around once.

From space, most of the Earth looks blue.

Always in orbit

As the Earth is spinning, or rotating, it's also making its long, 365-day trip around the Sun. The planet travels fast, but we cannot feel the movement here on Earth.

Super satellites

Lots of special spacecraft called satellites orbit the Earth. Satellites have many different jobs. They can take pictures, track the weather and help us use TV, telephones and radios.

There are **thousands** of man-made satellites.

Earth is wrapped in a thin blanket of gases.

What a view!

From the Moon, Earth is an impressive sight. Astronauts often describe it as the 'Blue Marble' because of all the water that covers its surface. Clouds of water vapour make the planet appear to shine.

Blast off!

In order to explore the Solar System, astronauts have to travel outside the Earth's atmosphere. They use rocket power to launch spacecraft, satellites and probes up into space.

Whoosh!

Sun

The Sun is a star, just like the ones that we see in the night sky. The burning ball of gas is much closer to Earth than any other stars, so it looks much bigger and brighter. The Sun is close enough to Earth for us to feel its warmth.

The Sun is so bright, we shouldn't look straight at it.

Golden glow

Without the Sun, there wouldn't be any life on Earth – our planet would be dark and frozen and wouldn't have any plants or animals. Living things need the Sun's light, heat and energy to survive and grow.

Did you know?

The Sun was made around 4.5 billion years ago. It was formed out of an enormous cloud of gas and dust that slowly got pressed together by gravity.

Spots and flares

The Sun's gases move and flow as they burn. This creates dark and lighter patches on the star's surface. The dark areas are giant storms. There are also huge explosions called solar flares.

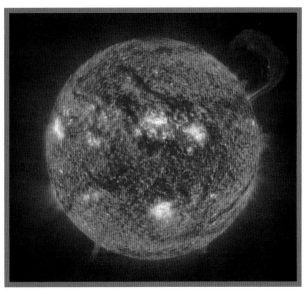

Solar flares look like bright spots on the Sun's surface.

Mega star

Although it looks small in the sky, the Sun is actually much bigger than Earth. In fact, the Sun is about a million times larger than our planet. If the Earth were the size of a pinhead, the Sun would be as big as a football!

One of many

The Sun is special to us, but it is just one of many stars. There are billions more in our galaxy! Compared to them, the Sun is not even very large.

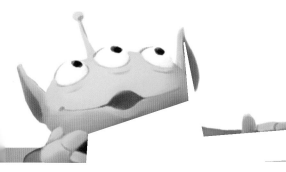

A group of stars is called a **cluster**.

Moon

Some planets, including Earth, have moons travelling around them. Our Moon is a rocky ball that circles Earth once every 27 days. It is a cold, dusty place without water or air. Only 12 people have ever walked on its surface.

From Earth, we can only see one side of the Moon.

Light of the Moon?

When you see the Moon at night, it looks silvery and bright, but the Moon doesn't give off any light of its own. It is actually a dull grey colour! It looks almost white to us because it reflects light from the Sun.

A lunar footprint.

Did you know?

There is no wind or rain on the Moon. Footprints left by visitors could stay undisturbed for millions of years!

Changing phases

As the Moon travels around the Earth, the Sun shines on it at different angles, changing the way it looks in the sky. It can look like a circle, a semicircle or even a crescent.

A **crescent** moon.

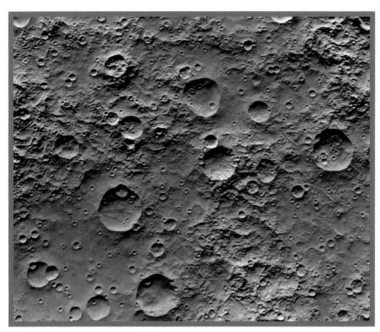

Craters dotted across the Moon's surface.

Craters and seas

The surface of the Moon has many deep holes, called craters. Parts of it are also covered by lava from old volcanoes that has cooled down and gone hard. These areas are called seas.

Many moons away

Six of the eight planets in our Solar System also have one or more moons. Mars has 2, Neptune has 14, Uranus has 27 and Saturn has 62! Jupiter has 67 that we know of, and new ones are being discovered all the time.

Io is one of Jupiter's moons.

Planets

The planets in our Solar System come in all shapes and sizes. Some are covered with volcanoes, some rage with storms, while others have colourful rings around them.

Mercury

Starting small

Mercury is the closest planet to the Sun, even though it is still a huge distance away! Mercury travels around the Sun faster than any other planet in our Solar System.

Hot rock

Venus is the only planet in the Solar System that spins in the opposite direction to Earth. It also spins very slowly. Venus has more volcanoes than the other planets. Scientists are not sure if they will erupt again in the future.

Venus

Jupiter

Mars

The Red Planet

Mars is called the 'Red Planet' because of its rocky, orange-red soil. It is known to have many dust storms. This makes the sky on Mars always look pink or pale orange in colour.

Neptune

Distant world

Of all the planets, Neptune has the wildest weather! It has massive storms and the most powerful winds in the Solar System. Neptune is a huge gas giant. A gas called methane has made the surface blue in colour.

Uranus

Side spinner

Uranus is the third largest planet in the Solar System. It looks like a smooth, round ball tilted on its side. There are light rings around its middle. Uranus is so far away, it can be very difficult to see without a telescope.

Saturn

Super circles

Saturn is a large gas planet known for its amazing rings. The rings are made up of ice, dust and pieces of rock. This planet takes about 30 Earth years to revolve around the Sun.

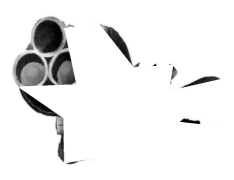

The gas giant

Jupiter is the largest planet in the Solar System. It is so big that 1,300 Earths could fit inside it! Jupiter has a 'Great Red Spot' on its surface. This is actually a huge, hurricane-like storm with fierce, swirling winds.

Astronauts

An astronaut is a person who travels into space to explore or work. There is no air to breathe in space, and it can be either extremely cold or burning hot. Astronauts have to wear a special suit to survive in these harsh conditions.

Helmet

Safe and sealed

A spacesuit seals an astronaut into a safe place so that he or she can do their job. It provides air to breathe, water to drink and equipment to control the temperature.

Eyes and ears

The helmet has a large visor so that the astronaut can see clearly. It has a built-in camera to record what the astronaut is seeing and doing.

Life support system

Gloves

Boots

Communication controls

Space school

Astronauts have to do lots of training before they are ready to go on a space mission. In space there is very little gravity, so it is important for astronauts to practise being weightless.

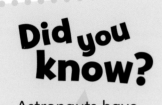

In space, there is no up or down.

Life in space

The International Space Station is a giant spacecraft that orbits the Earth. Many countries helped to build it. A team of astronauts stay on-board for months at a time, working together to find out more about space.

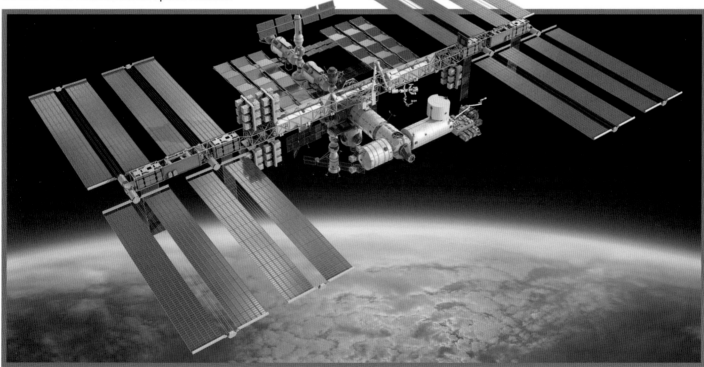

Model of the International Space Station.

Space vehicles

Spacecraft are vehicles and machines that are made to travel outside of the Earth's atmosphere. The first rockets went into orbit over 50 years ago. Since then scientists have been able to build even better, more advanced craft.

A stamp showing the first men on the Moon.

Space firsts

In 1961, Russian Yuri Gagarin was the first person to go into space. American astronaut, Neil Armstrong, was the first person to walk on the Moon in 1969.

Leap!

The **space shuttle** could land like an aeroplane.

Space shuttles

The space shuttle was the first reusable spacecraft. It could carry astronauts and cargo up into space and then return them to Earth once they had finished their mission.

Space probes

Special spacecraft called probes are launched into space to explore distant planets and stars. They don't have astronauts on-board. Instead they are controlled by scientists on Earth, who study the pictures and information that they send back.

The Russian Soyuz rocket blasts off.

What next?

Scientists are developing new technology all of the time. Many believe that space travel in the future will be easier and cheaper. It might not be too long before humans can even go on holiday in space!

Index